NEW ZEALAND
THE ULTIMATE EXPERIENCE

GW00726756

Photographs by

Mark Baynham, Mike Bhana, Peter Bush, Anthony Corban, Paul Daly, Cam Feast, Conon Fraser, Arno Gasteiger, Matt Greenslade, Richard Hare, Sheena Haywood, Martin Hill, Mike Hollman, Roger Jarrett, John King, Brian Latham, Richard Linton, Grant Masterton, Anthony Phelps, Nathan Secker, Wayne Tait, Dick Roberts, Ralph Talmont, Kaz Tanabe and Jenner Zimmermann.

David Bateman

Northland, the subtropical tip of the North Island, where sandy dunes (Te Paki, far right) and ancient forests are the major features of the landscape, is an area steeped in Maori legend and more recent history of European settlement. Kauri gum (bottom), a resinous substance sourced from the great kauri pines (Waipoua, right), was exported to Europe and America well into this century.

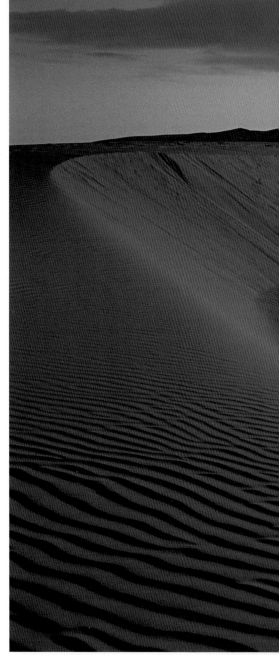

The town of Russell (bottom) in the Bay of Islands was the first capital of the new British colony.
An important trading and whaling centre in the past, it is now a spectacular haven for boating and big game fishing enthusiasts. Piercy Island (top), complete with its "Hole in the Rock", is one of dozens strewn throughout the bay.

Pompallier House, built by the first Catholic bishop in the south-west Pacific to house a mission station and a printing press, has been extensively renovated. It stands on a piece of land bought by the bishop from a local liquor salesman in 1839 and is one of the few original buildings left standing after a turbulent colonial past.

Auckland's many extinct volcanoes have become symbols of the city. Sheep graze on the slopes of One Tree Hill (far left) and other volcanic cones, most of which were fortified villages (pa) in pre-European times. Auckland Institute and Museum (left) houses a large collection of Maori and Polynesian arts and crafts, in addition to historical, ethnographic and scientific displays.

The capital of New Zealand from 1840 to 1865, Auckland is effectively the country's main commercial centre and home to a third of its population. The city is situated on a picturesque natural harbour so sailing is a favourite past-time but other outdoor pursuits such as golf, sea kayaking and even hot air ballooning are popular.

West coast beaches such as
Muriwai (right), at the foot of
the Waitakere Ranges, have
been described as stark and
wild but their appeal is
unrivalled.
The gannet colony at
Muriwai (bottom right) is one
of only two mainland
colonies in the country and
is as popular with tourists as
it is with the locals.

Walking and mountain bike tracks weave through the Waitakeres (left) which cradle the western side of the city.
Rangitoto Island (following pages) is Auckland's youngest volcano, with vegetation still in the process of reclaiming its lava slopes.

From a remote mid 19th century mission outpost, Tauranga has grown into a major regional centre and an important fishing and cargo port. A relaxed atmosphere prevails, however, and Tauranga has also become a favourite retirement spot.

Mt Maunganui (bottom) has been a much-loved holiday destination for generations of New Zealanders.
The summit, once a Maori fortress, offers an unequalled view over the Bay of Plenty and out towards the fuming volcano of White Island. Surfers enjoy the seaward side of the peninsula while the harbour side offers calmer waters.

Hawke's Bay is historically the most important wine region in New Zealand. Mission Vineyards (top left), established by French missionaries in 1851, is one of some thirty wineries in the area and the oldest one in the country still under the same management — the Society of St Mary. The area as a whole is especially prized for its reds and Chardonnays.

Rebuilt after a devastating earthquake in 1931, which dramatically changed much of Hawke's Bay's topography, Napier is now a small gem of Art Deco architecture (top left and left). An Art Deco festival, held each February, draws architecture enthusiasts from all over the world.

An unearthly blue/green light is emitted by the larvae of the glow worm, suspended from the ceiling of a cave in Waitomo (left).

Overlooking the western coast of the North Island, Mt Taranaki (Mt Egmont), protrudes from the otherwise flat agricultural land and is a reference point for the entire Taranaki region.

Rotorua's Tudor-style bath house, built to accommodate growing numbers of spa-goers last century, is now a regional museum. Theme parks Rainbow Springs (bottom) and Agrodome, both a short distance from Rotorua, stage regular and popular agricultural demonstrations.

Clive Fugill, master carver at Rotorua's Maori Arts and Crafts Institute, is completing a carving of a canoe sternpost. A lacquer finish will be applied to the finished work. Carving in wood, as well as bone and greenstone, is a major artistic tradition of the Maori, with carvings representing genealogical and mythological themes.

Hongi (right) or "sharing of breath" is a traditional Maori greeting and symbolises friendship. The gate to Rotorua's Whakarewarewa thermal reserve and model village (far right) depicts the semi-legendary lovers Hinemoa and Tutanekai. The village offers visitors a look at the layout of a traditional settlement and includes displays of food stores, sleeping quarters and a fine meeting house.

The thermal area of hot springs, boiling lakes and fumaroles forms a rough triangle in the centre of the North Island. One of only three major geyser groupings in the world, it is the subject of many myths and a valuable source of geothermal energy. Waiotapu (right) and Waimangu Valley reserves (bottom left and right) are only a short distance from Rotorua.

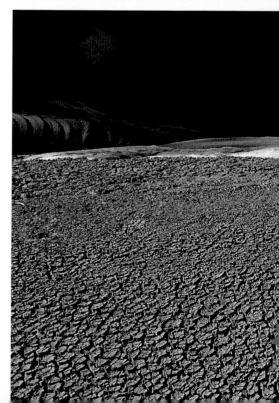

Central North Island is also one of the world's favourite trout fishing spots. Lakes Taupo, Rotorua and Tarawera (left) tempt anglers with a mix of great fishing and beautiful scenery. Brown trout catches above ten pounds are considered trophy material, destined for the taxidermist rather than the frying pan, but even fourteen-pounders are not uncommon.

Mt Ngauruhoe peeps through a snow sculpture (right) created on top of Mt Ruapehu by environmental artist Martin Hill only days before a major Ruapehu eruption (far right). Huka Falls (bottom), where the Waikato River descends eleven metres through a rocky canyon, are among the most spectacular waterfalls in the country.

Wellington, established in the 1830s, became New Zealand's capital in 1865. These days a single house parliament sits in the curiously shaped building aptly named the "Beehive", built beside the original parliament buildings.

From the house-clad hills which surround the inner city and Lambton Quay, a cable car descends past the Botanic Gardens and through tunnels to the commercial centre of Wellington.

Pancake Rocks at Punakaiki, at the northern end of the West Coast, (right) are made of limestone deposits. Further south, Lake Mahinapua (far right) is one of several mirror-like lakes along the West Coast. Glaciers are another feature of the area. Both the Fox Glacier (bottom right) and neighbouring Franz Josef Glacier have been advancing since about 1991.

Designed by Sir George Gilbert Scott, the Christchurch Cathedral (top right) was built of local stone and consecrated in 1881. It is a fine example of Gothic revival architecture. Trams (bottom right), many years ago part of the city's public transport system, are now in use as a tourist attraction.

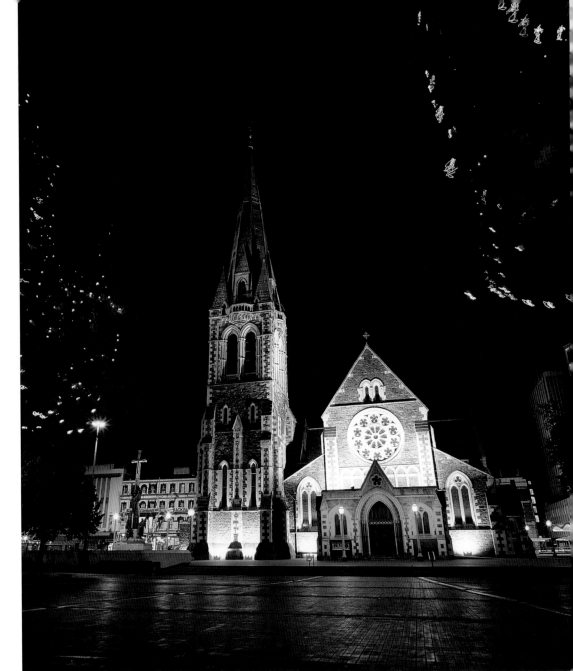

The Avon River (left) meanders its way seaward through the heart of Christchurch.
Situated close to the Botanic Gardens, the Canterbury Museum (top) is noted for its local and national collections, which include an Antarctic display.

Christchurch lives up to its name — the "Garden City", as evidenced by the city's parks and the elegant Botanic Gardens (right). Akaroa, a charming town on Banks Peninsula near Christchurch (bottom), was home to French settlers in the 19th century. Much of the French flavour remains, with street names like Rue Viard.

Tekapo's Church of the Good Shepherd (right) is a Mackenzie Country landmark. Its isolation in the landscape is symbolic of the early days of settlement.
Burke Pass (bottom), the northern entrance to the Mackenzie Country, was named after an early explorer.

Mount Cook (from The Hermitage, following pages) rises 3754 metres above the Tasman and Hooker glaciers. Its summit has posed a frequent challenge to mountaineers and adventurers, especially since a massive avalanche in 1991 made its eastern face even more difficult.

Rippon Vineyard on Lake Wanaka (bottom) and Gibbston Valley Wines (left) are just two of the local wineries which take advantage of the area's continental climate.
Local Pinot Noir is particularly good.
Thrills of a more physical nature await those keen enough to board a jet boat for a ride on the Shotover River (far left).

Central Otago was the scene of several large gold rushes last century. Prospectors from all over the world flocked to the area (including Skippers Canyon, bottom) in search of fortune. As a result, many settlements (including Arrowtown, right) were founded. At the height of the rush, tens of thousands of miners struggled to survive and, sometimes, prosper in the unforgiving terrain.

These days adventurers in Central Otago seek adrenalin through other pursuits: bungy jumping into deep canyons (Kawarau Gorge, far left) or skiing on any of a range of ski fields such as Coronet Peak (left). A speedy gondola ride takes visitors to the top of Queenstown's Bob's Peak (bottom left) with views over the town, Lake Wakatipu and surrounding mountains.

Queenstown is one of the
most popular destinations
in the country. Innumerable
visitors have enjoyed cross-
ing Lake Wakatipu on the
steamer Earnslaw
(far right), in the shadow of
the magnificent mountain
range known as The
Remarkables. Millbrook
Lodge (right) offers golfers
from all over the world an
opportunity to play in a
spectacular setting.

"The best walk in the world", four-day Milford Track (far left) crosses the Mackinnon Pass to the Arthur Valley and offers a mix of alpine and bush scenery. Fiordland National Park has many popular tracks (including the Hollyford, left). Everywhere mischievous keas (bottom left) are quick to demonstrate their curious personality.

Lake Te Anau (right) is one of many glacial lakes in Fiordland. Across the lake from the township the famous glow-worm caves can be visited. Waterfalls, bird life and several fur seal colonies can be seen from charter vessels cruising the Milford Sound (far right). Following pages: Snow-capped in the winter months, Mitre Peak marks the halfway point of the Sound.

New Zealand has over two hundred species of fern. It is not surprising then that the koru or young fern form (right) has found its way into Maori art, such as a carving adorning a waka or canoe (far right), and become one of the symbols of the country.

Published in 1996 by David Bateman Ltd, Tarndale Grove, Albany, Auckland, New Zealand.

Reprinted 2005

Copyright © David Bateman Ltd, 1996.
Photographs © individual photographers.

This book is copyright. Except for the purpose of fair review, no part may be stored or transmitted in any form or by any means, electronic or mechanical, including recording or storage in any information retrieval system without permission in writing from the publisher.

No reproduction may be made, whether by photocopying or by any other means, unless a licence has been obtained from the publisher or its agent.

Edited by Ralph Talmont

Produced by Mandragora, Box 68582, Newton, Auckland, New Zealand.

Captions by Lyn Anderson

Thanks to Mike Warren at Möbius, Richard Hare at Lightworks and Tim Warren and Ae Sook Sim at Visual Impact for their assistance.

Printed in China through Colorcraft Ltd., Hong Kong

ISBN 1 86953 2902

Photographic credits:
Cover: Krzysztof Pfeiffer, 2-3: Brian Latham, 4-5: John King, 6-7: Richard Hare, 8-9: Arno Gasteiger (3), 10-11: top – Cam Feast, right – Mike Hollman, bottom – Fotopress, 12-13: Krzysztof Pfeiffer (2), 14-15: left – Ralph Talmont, right – Krzysztof Pfeiffer, 16-17: left – Mike Bhana, top right – Jenner Zimmermann, bottom right – Kaz Tanabe, 18-19: Ralph Talmont, 20-21: top – Roger Jarrett, bottom – Wayne Tait, 22-23: top left – Ralph Talmont, top right – Fotopress, bottom – Fotopress, 24-25: left – Nathan Secker, right – Dick Roberts, 26-27: right and bottom left – Brian Latham, top left – Ralph Talmont, 28-29: left – Arno Gasteiger, right – Ralph Talmont, 30-31: Brian Latham (3), bottom right – Ralph Talmont, 32-33: top left – Conon Fraser, bottom left – Anthony Corban, right – Martin Hill, 34-35: top – Anthony Phelps, bottom – Peter Bush, 36-37: top – Matt Greenslade, bottom – Ralph Talmont, 38-39: Nathan Secker (3), 40-41: Ralph Talmont, 42-43: top left and right – Ralph Talmont, bottom left – Mike Hollman, 44-45: top – Grant Masterton, bottom – Ralph Talmont, 46-47: top left and top right – Richard Hare, bottom left – Paul Daly, bottom right – Richard Linton, 48-49: Nathan Secker (2), 50-51: top – Mike Hollman, bottom – Ralph Talmont, 52-53: Ralph Talmont, 54-55: top right and bottom – Ralph Talmont, top left – Richard Linton, 56-57: Nathan Secker (2), 58-59: left – Fotopress, top right – Sheena Haywood, bottom right – Ralph Talmont, 60-61: left – Nathan Secker, right – Paul Daly, 62-63: left and top right – Sheena Haywood, bottom right – Ralph Talmont, 64-65: right – Mark Baynham, left – Mikc Hollman, 66-67: Mike Hollman, 68-69: top – Ralph Talmont, bottom – Richard Hare, 70-71: left – Richard Linton, right – Brian Latham, 72: top – Richard Hare, centre – Ralph Talmont.

All photographers except Krzysztof Pfeiffer, Fotopress, Martin Hill and Dick Roberts are represented by Visual Impact Pictures, Box 8337, Symonds Street, Auckland, Telephone 09 307 6757.